THE MAPLE SYRUP MAFIA

A HISTORY OF ORGANIZED CRIME IN CANADA

ORGANIZED CRIME SERIES #7

GREG THOMPSON

Absolute Crime Press

ANAHEIM, CALIFORNIA

ABSO UTE CR ME

www.AbsoluteCrime.com

Contents

ABOUT ABSOLUTE CRIME

Absolute Crime publishes only the best true crime literature. Our focus is on the crimes that you've probably never heard of, but you are fascinated to read more about. With each engaging and gripping story, we try to let readers relive moments in history that some people have tried to forget.

Remember, our books are not meant for the faint at heart. We don't hold back--if a crime is bloody, we let the words splatter across the page so you can experience the crime in the most horrifying way!

If you enjoy this book, please visit our homepage (www.AbsoluteCrime.com) to see other books we offer; if you have any feed-

back, we'd love to hear from you!

Sign up for our mailing list, and we'll send

you out a free true crime book!

http://www.absolutecrime.com/newsletter

INTRODUCTION

Even though they are separate countries with very different histories and governments, the United States and Canada share the same economy. Many businesses operate on both sides of the border, including organized crime.

The Mafia is no exception: Canada's Italian crime families are as large and as powerful as any in the United States. They also have a reputation for violence and corruption that rivals their counterparts south of the border.

Like the American Mafia, Canada's mob has historically been centered in urban areas with a large Italian population. In Canada, this means the provinces of Ontario and Quebec and the nation's two largest cities, Toronto and Montreal, both of which are located a short distance from the U.S. border.

The origins of the modern Canadian Mafia can be traced to the 1940s and '50s and the beginnings of the international drug trade. The increasing demand for heroin coincided with a surge of Italian immigration into Canada. Most of the immigrants were honest and hardworking citizens, but as in the U.S., a small core of hardened gangsters from Sicily and Italy came to the New World in search of opportunity.

CHAPTER 1: THE MONTREAL CONNECTION – THE MAFIA IN QUEBEC

The Canadian city most associated with the Mafia is Montreal, which is home to two of Canada's best known mob families. Montreal has also seen plenty of mob violence, including several bloody gang wars and numerous Mafia hits. Much of this violence stemmed from

Montreal's close proximity to the Northeastern and Midwestern U.S., which made it a natural drug conduit.

THE RIZZUTOS: THE SIXTH FAMILY

The most famous crime family in Montreal is the Rizzutos, who are closely connected with New York's Bonanno crime family, one of the legendary Five Families that forms the top level of the American Mafia. Interestingly, the American Federal Bureau of Investigation (FBI) considers the Rizzutos a Canadian offshoot of the Bonnanos, while the Royal Canadian Mounted Police (RCMP) think the Rizzutos are an independent organization. Some mob scholars have went as far as to label the Rizzutos "the Sixth Family", which means they have as much influence in the underworld as their New York brethren.

The Rizzuto Family began in February 1954 when Nicolo and Libertina Rizzuto emigrated from poverty-stricken Sicily to Canada. Nicolo and Libertina were looking for a better life in Canada for their eight-year-old son Vito. Nicolo Rizzuto certainly found wealth, power, and success in Canada as the founder and leader of a powerful mob family.

The Rizzutos settled in Montreal, and newspaper reports indicate that Nicolo quickly set himself up as a force to be reckoned with in the local underworld. The Rizzutos were certainly in the right time and the right place; Montreal was a major conduit in the legendary French Connection, the heroin pipeline from the Mediterranean to the American Heartland. There was big money to made moving heroin, particularly for experienced gangsters with connections in Italy and France.

It is highly likely that Nicolo Rizzuto moved to Montreal specifically to engage in the drug trade. He arrived in the city one year after mobsters Vic "the Egg" Cotroni and Carmine Galante, the boss of the Bonnano's, one of New York's five mob families, opened a major heroin pipeline through Montreal. Rizzuto and other Sicilian mobsters might have been sent to Montreal to oversee the heroin business because the Sicilians didn't trust the Cotronis, who were from Calabria in southern Italy, not Sicily.

By the time he moved to Montreal, Nicolo was already a hardened mobster. He was already married to a mob boss's daughter back in Sicily. Nicolo's father, another Mafiosi, had moved to New York in 1925 and been killed there in 1933.

Like a good Italian boy, Vito Rizzuto attended St. Pius X, a Catholic high school, while his father and uncle built up the family business. Nicolo wasn't yet the big boss in Montreal, but he was building up a powerful Mafia crew. By 1974, the crew was so powerful that rumors that Vic the Egg and his right hand man, Palo Violi, wanted to eliminate Nicolo were floating around town. Fearing for his life and hoping to avoid prosecution, Nicolo fled to Venezuela and left Vito in charge.

Vito first attracted police attention in 1978 when Palo Violi, who was the likely successor to Cotroni family boss Vic Cotroni, was rubbed out. The Cotroni family, which was then Montreal's most powerful criminal group, was made up of immigrants from Calabria in southern

Italy. The Cotronis were also closely connected with mob families in Ontario.

Even though the FBI and RCMP both identified Vito as the man who ordered Paolo Violi blown away with a shotgun in 1978, he was never charged with the crime. Three Sicilian immigrants, including Vito's uncle, Domenico Manno, did plead guilty to the crime.

Nicolo Rizzuto made good use of his sojourn in South America, where he was the guest of the powerful local Mafia family, the Cunteras. During his absence, he set up a drug pipeline that brought Colombian cocaine to Montreal via Venezuela. He also organized a similar network that moved cocaine to Mafia families in Western Europe.

The elimination of the Violis turned Montreal into the Rizzuto family's playground. With Violi dead, Nicolo activated the connections he had set up. The father and son team quickly turned the Port of Montreal into one of the largest drug importation centers in North America. Their imports included hashish from Pakistan and Lebanon, cocaine from Colombia, and heroin from Sicily and Thailand.

The Rizzutos had organized a sophisticated international smuggling network overseen from Venezuela by Nicolo. Vito called the shots in Montreal, while Nicolo ran the entire organization from South America.

The major customers for the drugs were Mafia families in New York and New Jersey. The Rizzutos even had their own man in New York, Gerlando Sciascia, who kept John Gotti's crew and other New York mob outfits well-supplied with drugs.

The close relations with New York were both profitable, but dangerous. The huge drug profits to be made in the city led to mob warfare and dragged the Rizzutos into it. Vito and Sciascia got friendly with New York by doing the Bonnano family's dirty work.

Court testimony indicates that on May 5, 1981, Sciascia invited three mobsters, Alphonse Indelicato, Philip Giaccone and Dominick Trinchera, who were known to be plotting against the Bonnano family leadership, to a "social club" in Brooklyn. When the three entered the club, four men that allegedly included Vito Rizzuto shot them dead with pistols.

The killings put Rizzuto's associates in charge in New York and left the drug pipeline wide open. The Rizzuto organization was now able to import drugs from all over the world and sell them to dealers in large cities throughout the U.S. and Canada. They also branched out into other kinds of crime.

Law enforcement sources indicate that Vito Rizzuto attempted to smuggle gold into Canada that Ferdinand and Imelda Marcos, the former President and First Lady of the Philippines, had stolen from their country's treasury. There is also evidence that he was involved in stock scams and a giant counterfeiting operation.

Money laundering was another hugely lucrative racket for the Rizzutos. The RCMP estimated that $91 million in cash moved through one of Rizzuto's laundries in just four years.

Even though Rizzuto's activities were well known, the RCMP and local police were unable to make a case against him. Rizzuto was even labeled Canada's "Teflon Don" by the media, a reference to his flashy American associate, John Gotti. Media accounts indicate that

Rizzuto was more Teflon than Gotti; he evaded arrest and prosecution far longer than his counterpart in Queens.

Nicolo wasn't so lucky; he was arrested for drug trafficking in Venezuela in 1988 and sentenced to eight years in prison. The elder Rizzuto was released in 1993 after serving five years and returned to Montreal.

Part of the reason why Rizzuto got away with it for so long was that the police were busy with other more colorful criminals, namely outlaw biker gangs. The notorious Quebec Biker War was raging and the police had little time for old school mobsters while the outlaws were soaking the streets with blood. Unlike the Rizzutos, the bikers were home grown, and they attracted more attention. The bikers were also far more violent, so the police considered them a bigger menace.

BROUGHT DOWN BY THE FBI

Vic Rizzuto's power in Montreal continued unchecked, even as the FBI was able to demolish the New York Mafia and send many of its leaders, including John Gotti, to prison. It was the downfall of the Bonnano family that eventually ended Vic's career.

In 2004, FBI informants fingered Vic Rizzuto as the leader of the hit squad that took out Indelicato, Trinchera, and Giaccone in 1981. Vic was arrested, deported to the United States, and tried for the murders. Vic was eventually convicted and imprisoned in Supermax, the toughest federal prison in the U.S., located in Florence, Colo.

The rats who took down Vic Rizzuto may have included Big Joe Massino, who was the boss of the Bonnano family. Massino's testimony brought down several members of the family, including his successor, "Vinny Gorgeous" Basciano, in 2005.

Nicolo Rizzuto went down again in 2006 when the RCMP succeeded in hiding cameras and microphones in his favorite hangout, the Consenza Social Club. Rizzuto was among 70 mobsters caught discussing drug trafficking and other crimes on tape. Nicolo, then 84, pleaded guilty to racketeering in September 2008 and received three years' probation for his involvement. The judge insisted that Nicolo stay under house arrest, but he was allowed to go out for the funeral of his grandson, Vito Rizzuto Jr.

Vic and Nicolo's removals triggered an all-gang war in Montreal between the Irish gangs, the Hells Angels, various Mafia factions, street gangs, and even Colombian drug cartels. The Rizzuto's enemies were so emboldened that they took to throwing Molotov cocktails at Italian cafes and other Mafia hangouts around Montreal.

When Vic went to prison, veteran Mafiosi Agostino Cuntera took over the Rizzuto organization. Cuntera was a third-generation Mafia member born in Sicily in 1944. Cuntera was closely connected to many Mafia families by the thickest ties of all, blood. His brothers ran the Venezuelan end of the Colombia to Montreal drug connection. Cuntera also had connections to the powerful Caruana family, which operated one of the world's most profitable drug trafficking networks.

Like Nicolo Rizzuno, Cuntera was probably sent to Montreal by the Sicilian Mafia to look after its interests in the city. He rose through the ranks and earned the Rizzutos' loyalty by helping kill Paolo Violi with a shotgun, the act that cleared the way for a Sicilian takeover in Montreal. Cuntera maintained the code of silence and pleaded guilty to the crime to cover for Vic Rizzuto.

During the 1990s, Rizzuto had attracted some attention for his friendship with a local politician named Alfonso Gagliano, who was also a Sicilian and a prominent member of the then powerful Liberal Party. Media articles eventually exposed the relationship.

The growing mob war made Cuntera so nervous that he began riding around in an armored car with a bodyguard. The armored car didn't do him any good; gunmen simply waited until Cuntera and his bodyguard got out of the car and shot them outside a food supply warehouse on June 30, 2010.

The other casualties of the war included Vito Rizzuto Jr., who was shot in the face in his car on Dec. 28, 2009, Nicolo Rizzuto, who was killed by a sniper in his mansion on Nov. 10, 2010, and Vito's brother-in-law, Paolo Renda, who was reportedly kidnapped from his house in May 2010. Renda's body has never been found, so there is a possibility that he might be alive in the Witness Protection Program or in hiding somewhere.

The Rizzutos retaliated for the killings in November 2011 by rubbing out Salvatore "Sal the Iron Worker" Montagna, who was the acting boss of the Bonnano family. Sal, who had been born in Montreal, but raised in Sicily, was reportedly trying to combine the Bonnanos and Rizzutos into one multinational crime family. Sal had been deported to Montreal a year before the killing. Montagna was deported because he was a convicted felon and ineligible to stay in the U.S.

Once back in his birthplace, Sal tried to take over the Rizzuto family's rackets by killing its members. In true old school Mafia fashion, the Iron Worker's body was found on the shores of the L'Assomption River with a bullet in it on Nov. 24, 2011. Oddly enough, investigators don't think the body was dumped; instead, they think Montagna jumped in the river to escape a Rizzuto family hit squad.

Police have arrested several suspects in Montagna's murder, including Raynald Desjardins, who has been described as Vito Rizzuto's right-hand man. Two months before Montagna's death, Desjardins escaped a murder attempt near his home.

Interestingly enough, Vito Rizzuto survived the mob war by serving time in Supermax. He was released from Supermax in October 2012. It remains to be seen if he will try to take control of the Sixth Family and Montreal again.

If he returns to Montreal, Rizzuto may not have long to live. In early November, just a few weeks after Rizzuto walked out of Supermax, Raynald Desjardins' brother-in-law, Joe Di-Maulo, was shot down in his driveway. It isn't clear who killed Desjardins, but somebody might be trying to finish off the Rizzutos once and for all.

THE COTRONI FAMILY – MONTREAL'S ORIGINAL MOB

The Canadian Mafia, like its American counterpart, is divided into factions from the island of Sicily and Calabria in southern Italy. Although the Sicilians, led by the Rizzutos, are the most powerful Italian crime faction in Canada, they have had many battles with the Calabrians. Interestingly enough, the Calabrians are not technically part of the Mafia; instead, they are historically associated with the Ndrangheta, a rival criminal secret society based in Calabria (La Cosa Nostra Database).

The main Calabrian faction in Montreal is the Cotroni crime family, which was in operation before the Rizzutos left Sicily. Unlike the Rizzutos, the Cotronis concentrated their activities in Canada and attempted to expand to Toronto. Even though they were major drug importers, the Cotronis were also heavily involved with many local rackets, such as gambling, loansharking, protection, and various scams related to political corruption.

The Cotroni family was established by Vic "the Egg" Cotroni, who was born in Calabria in 1911. Vic came to Montreal in 1924 when his parents immigrated to Canada. As his name implies, Vic Cotroni was a colorful character who worked as a professional wrestler before going into organized crime. Among other things, the Egg was once charged with the rape of a woman named Maria Bresciano, but the charges were dropped when Maria married him. Another interesting fact about Vic Cotroni was that he reportedly never learned how to read and write, although it should be noted that Cotroni may have been able to do both in Italian because he lived in that country until he was 13.

The Egg entered the big time through his connection with Bonanno family boss Carmine Galante. In 1953, Galante set up the first heroin connection through Montreal and put the Egg in charge of it. By 1957, the Cotroni family was so powerful that Vic's younger brother, Frank, represented the family at the Appalachian Conference, a summit meeting of mobsters from all over North America.

The heroin trade and other rackets made Vic Cotroni a very wealthy man. He lived in true Mafia fashion, building a palatial home in the suburb of Lavaltrie that had marble floors, a conference room, a walk-in refrigerator, and a built-in movie theater in the 1960s. Like Al Capone, Cotroni tried to buy respect by donating large amounts of money to local churches.

Something Vic hated was publicity, which he got when the Canadian magazine McLean's printed an article exposing him as Montreal's "godfather." Interestingly enough, Cotroni didn't have the reporter whacked; instead, he sued McLean's for $1.25 million. Cotroni won the suit, but the judge reduced the settlement to just $2.

The Egg was finally arrested in 1974 after he and associate Palo Violi were heard threatening to kill Johnny Papalia, the mob boss for Hamilton, Ontario, on a wiretap. All three men were later arrested, tried, convicted, and sent to prison. Three years later, Violi and Cotroni were released because Papalia was still alive.

Cotroni eventually died of cancer in 1984 and was the object of an elaborate funeral. The funeral entourage featured 23 cars and a 17-piece brass band.

The Cotroni family's position in the Montreal underworld had already been taken by the Rizzutos by the time of Vic Cotroni's death. The Rizzutos were able to cement their power in Montreal because they had eliminated the one Calabrian monster capable of resisting their power grab, Paolo Violi.

Violi was born in Sinopoli, Italy, in 1933, but moved to Hamilton, Ontario with his family in the early 1950s. By 1955, Violi was a hardened criminal who had committed a murder. He beat the rap by claiming self-defense because the man had allegedly pulled a knife on him.

Violi moved to Montreal in the 1960s where he caught the eye of Frank (or Giuseppe) Cotroni, the Egg's younger brother. Frank asked Violi to take over the counterfeiting and bootlegging rackets. Violi brought his brothers, Francesco and Rocco, in to help him run the rackets. Violi so impressed the Cotronis that he was considered Vic Cotroni's right-hand man and probable successor.

Violi soon became a victim of the ethnic and regional differences between Sicilian and Calabrian gangsters. The Cotronis' patrons in New York, the Sicilian-controlled Bonnano family, sided with the rising Rizzuto family in a growing battle for control of Montreal. The Rizzutos were Sicilian, and loyalty to the home island trumped business connections.

On Jan. 22, 1978, Paolo Violi's face was blown away with a shotgun while playing cards at a Montreal café. He died on the scene, and the Cotroni family's future died with him. Violi's brother and henchman, Francesco, was killed by Rizzuto's gunmen one year earlier. In 1980, the last of the Violi brothers, Rocco, was killed by a sniper while reading the newspaper.

Paolo Violi might have been murdered earlier if it were not for the fact that he was in prison. Violi only managed to live for two more years because he was serving time for threatening Johnny Papalia with Vic the Egg. Violi might have been able to avoid assassination if he had simply left Montreal and stayed away. He did not; he stayed in plain sight.

Three Rizzuto family members eventually pleaded guilty to the murder. Although the man the FBI and RCMP identified as the mastermind behind the killing, Rizzuto boss Vito Rizzuto was never charged.

The Cotroni family survived into the 1980s, but it was a poor shadow of its former self. It was able to operate local rackets, but without support from the Bonannos, it couldn't control the drug trade. Instead, it concentrated on local crimes and had to deal with challenges from other criminal groups.

CHAPTER 2: THE MAFIA AND THE QUEBEC BIKER WAR

The biggest challenge came from outlaw biker gangs, such as the Rock Machine and the Hells Angels. The Hells Angels moved into Montreal in 1977 when a local gang called the Popeyes linked up with them. By 1986, the Angels were so powerful that local drug dealers, including the notorious Dubois brothers, formed their own gang known as the Rock

Machine to fight the Angels. The dealers could no longer rely on the Cotronis for protection, so they took matters into their own hands.

By the 1990s, the Cotronis had lost complete control of the streets and an all-out war had broken out between the Hells Angels and the Rock Machine. When the Rock Machine couldn't match the numbers and firepower of the Hells Angels, they linked up with the Angels' archrivals, the Texas-based Bandidos.

The gang war, or Quebec Biker War, was one of the bloodiest in North American history and claimed as many as 150 lives and dragged on for 17 years, from 1992-2009. Violence escalated to the point that the bikers were setting off bombs and staging mass killings. The killings spread to Ontario and led to such outrages as the Lawrenceville Massacre, in which eight Bandidos were shot and dumped in a farmer's field near London, Ontario.

The Angels' ruthless tactics eventually helped them win the war. The Bandidos were so scared of the Angels that they called off their proposed expansion into Ontario. The war demonstrated that the Mafia was no longer in control in Montreal or Quebec. Instead, a new status quo in which the Sicilians functioned as drug smugglers and importers while the Bikers ran the streets prevailed.

The Biker War prompted the RCMP, popularly known as the Mounties, to focus most of its organized crime resources on the bikers. The Mounties eventually clamped down on the Hells Angels with a series of mass arrests in 2009. Almost the entire membership of the motorcycle gang in the provinces of Quebec and New Brunswick was rounded up. The

Mounties even went to the Dominican Republic and France to pick up Angels that had fled to those countries.

THE AFTERMATH OF THE BIKER WAR AND THE MONTREAL MAFIA'S UNCERTAIN FUTURE

Although the Mafia was not directly involved in the Biker War, the power vacuum it created on the streets might have led to the conflict between Sal "the Iron Worker" Montagna and the Rizzutos. Montanga might have been trying to take over the drug trade in the Angels' absence.

The end of the Biker War might also clear the way for another intriguing conflict, a battle between the Sicilian Mafia and the Hells Angels for control of Montreal. The killing of Raymand Desjardins might have been a message from the An (Humphreys, Calabrian Mafia boss earned mob's respect)gels to Vic Rizzuto to not resume his old activities. An even worse possibility would be that the Rizzutos manipulated the Bandidos/Rock Machine and Angels into launching the Biker War in (La Cosa Nostra Database) order to limit their power.

It is possible that the Angels and not Montagna might have been responsible for the deaths of Vic Rizzuto Jr., Nicolo Rizzuto, and Agostino Cuntera. Another possibility is that the bikers hired by Montagna committed the killings. If the Bikers were involved in the conflict, it opens up a whole new era in Quebec mob history.

The Biker War demonstrated that the Montreal Mafia is no longer the force it once was. The Cotroni crime family is history and the Rizzuto crime family is a pale shadow of its former self. The future of organized crime in Quebec probably belongs to home grown Canadian

criminals with powerful American allies such as

biker gangs rather than the Mafia.

CHAPTER 3: THE TORONTO AND HAMILTON CONNECTIONS – THE MAFIA IN ONTARIO

Ontario is Canada's largest and most important province. Southern Ontario can be regarded as the Canadian heartland and the center of the nation's economy. Not surprisingly, Ontario has attracted a lot of attention from the Mafia over the years.

The Mafia in Ontario is centered in the province's two most important cities: Canada's business center, Toronto, and the gritty old steel town of Hamilton. Control of Southern Ontario was important for the Mafia because it gave them access to Canada's largest markets for illegal goods. Southern Ontario also gave the mobsters control of lucrative smuggling routes to and from the nearby United States. Another big source of income for the Mafia in Canada is money laundering because of Canada's strict banking laws.

In recent decades cigarette smuggling has become one of the Canadian Mafia's most lucrative rackets. High taxes on cigarettes in Canada have created a large market for cheaper American smokes in the country. Much of the cigarette smuggling is done through

Native American reservations (called First Nations in Canada) along the U.S. border.

Although Italian gangsters were active in Ontario as early as the Prohibition era of the 1920s, the area didn't develop its own organized mob families until the 1950s. The Mafia emerged in the region because of an influx of Italian immigration and the growth of a lucrative illegal drug trade in the region.

THE MUSITANOS AND THE WAR FOR HAMILTON

The Hamilton-based Musitanos are considered a small Mafia family, yet they have a colorful and violent reputation. Like their rivals, such as the Siderno Group and the Papalia Family, the Musitanos' reach extended throughout Toronto and Southern Ontario and into nearby cities, such as Buffalo.

Little is known about the origins of the Musitano Family, but it is believed that it was formed in the 1950s by Dominic Musitano. For most of its history, the Musitano Family was content to work under Hamilton's colorful and violent mob boss, John Papalia. Papalia was a capo in the Magaddino crime family, based in Buffalo, New York. He was also a cousin of the Magaddino Family boss, Stefano Magaddino.

Like the Cotroni Family in Montreal and Toronto's Siderno Group, the Musitanos are technically not part of the Mafia. Instead, they are actually part of the Ndrangheta, another criminal organization based in Calabria, the region of Italy right next to Sicily. Even though it is a separate organization, the Ndrangheta works closely with the Mafia, particularly in its most lucrative business—drug trafficking.

"Johnny Pops," as Papalia was known, was one of North America's largest heroin importers. Among other things, he was heavily involved in the legendary French Connection, which brought heroin to the U.S. and Canada from Marseilles. Papalia was also one of the brains behind the pizza connection, in which Mafiosi set themselves up as small town pizzeria operators throughout the United States. The pizza restaurants were fronts for large scale heroin distribution.

It was Papalia, a second-generation mobster, more than anyone else who made Hamilton into a major mob town. Although he started his criminal career in burglary and illegal gambling, he soon graduated to big time drug dealing. By 1949, when he was arrested for selling heroin, Papalia was supplying up to a 1,000 addicts in Toronto with the drug. When he was arrested, Johnny Pops told the court he needed the drugs to treat his syphilis. Strangely, the judge fell for the claim (or for the bribe Papalia slipped him), and the gangster was sentenced to just two years in prison.

When he was released from prison in the early 1950s, Papalia was a good enough drug dealer to catch the eye of Bonnano Family bigwig, Carmine Galante. Galante, who was then managing the family's interests in Canada, recruited Papalia into the French Connection. Papalia worked closely with the Bonnano Family even though he was part of the Magaddino family.

He also worked closely with two other bigtime drug dealers, the Agueci brothers from Sicily, who were also working for the Bonnanos. The Agueci Brothers; Albert and Vito, controlled heroin distribution in Western New

York, Ohio, and Southern Ontario from their bakery in Toronto. Papalia was one of their top dealers until 1961 when Albert was tortured and strangled on Stefano Magaddino's orders. Albert's brutal killing cleared the way for Papalia to take over the heroin trade in Southern Ontario.

Even though he was one of the most powerful mobsters in Canada, Johnny Pops wasn't well liked. At one time Montreal mob boss, Vic Cotroni, and his chief henchman, Paolo Violi, were actually overheard threatening to kill Papalia on a wiretap. The two were eventually arrested, tried, and convicted for the incident and sentenced to six years in jail. They were eventually released because of the inconvenient fact that Papalia was still alive.

Nobody actually seemed to like Johnny Pops, but everybody in the mafia liked the huge amounts of cash he was bringing in. The two people who hated Papalia most were apparently two young mobsters named Pasquale and Angelo Musitano. Although their father had served Papalia loyally for decades and grown rich with him, the younger Musitanos wanted to take his place.

The Musitano brothers' father, Dominic, kept the two young hotheads under control until his death in 1995 of a heart attack. When Dominic died, the boys inherited the family business and started planning expansion, Mafia style. Their plans called for the elimination of Papalia and his right hand man, Carmen Barillaro. Both Papalia and Murdock were shot outside their own homes. The hit was reportedly carried out by a character named Ken Murdock. Murdock testified that his pay for killing Papalia was $2,000 and 40 grams of cocaine.

Murdock also reportedly shot Barillaro at his front door in Niagara Falls, Ontario.

The objective of the killings was apparently to make Pasquale or Pat Musitano the new boss of the Hamilton mafia. Chillingly, Pat Musitano was reportedly John Papalia's godson. The only thing that was achieved was to land both Musitano brothers in jail and to expose most of their operations to law enforcement and the media. What brought them down was their choice of a hit man.

Ken Murdock was obviously not the best choice for a hit man. He was quickly arrested by police and started spilling everything he knew about the crimes and the family. His testimony about the 1997 murders was so compelling that it caused Angelo and Pasquale Musitano to plead guilty to ordering the crime in 2000. The brothers were sentenced to ten years in prison but paroled after six years.

Angelo Musitano was arrested for a parole violation in 2007 when he was caught making contact with other criminals. He was apparently trying to carry on the family business but got caught. The parole violation might have been connected to an illegal gaming device according to an article in the National Post newspaper.

The Musitanos' efforts to build a mafia empire for themselves backfired badly. Organized crime expert and author, Antonio Nicaso, told reporter Adrian Humphreys that their killings of Barillaro and Papalia weakened the Mafia by ending the Magaddino family's control of Southern Ontario. It also removed the one Mafia figure capable of unifying the region's families and resisting outside groups like the Hells Angels.

Part of the reason for the killing might have been that the Musitano brothers were patriotic Canadians. The brothers might have resented the control of their rackets by an American mob family. Unlike their father, the Musitano brothers hated the idea of being under the heels of a U.S. organization. The elimination of Papalia cleared the way for the Toronto mafia to push the Buffalo family out of Southern Ontario once and for all so it achieved the brothers' goal of getting US mobsters out of Hamilton. It had some other effects that the Musitanos probably didn't want.

One result of the killing was allowing the Hells Angels to move into Southern Ontario. The bikers had kept out because "Johnny Pops" Papalia believed they were actually working for Montreal's Rizzuto Family. With Johnny Pops, who was also known as "The Enforcer," gone, the way was cleared for the outlaws to move in and take over.

The truth is that the Musitanos were never a full-fledged Mafia family; instead, they were a crew of the Papalia Family. Their attempt to become a real family was what eventually brought them down. They ended up demolishing the organization that John Papalia had created instead of taking it over.

Since 2007 the Musitano crew has apparently gone underground and let Toronto-based mob groups and the Hells Angels take over much of their territory. There has been no sign that the Musitanos are attempting to assert any sort of power over the Mailton-area rackets.

Ken Murdock only received 13 years in prison for the two murders. In 2009 he was released on parole with the stipulation that he would stay away from drugs. A year later Murdock's urine tested positive for cocaine—a clear parole violation. Murdock tried to keep from returning to prison by claiming that he was taking drugs to overcome anxiety caused by the appearance of his name and picture in newspapers. Parole officers didn't buy Murdock's excuse and sent him back to prison.

The authorities said there was no danger to Murdock despite his testimony against the Musitanos. Murdock himself had declined witness protection and even told a reporter that he was planning to move back to Hamilton and live under his own name. After getting out of jail, Murdock indicated that he would probably change his name.

While he was in prison, Murdock told another reporter that he had killed Papalia because another mobster owed Johnny Pops $250,000. He said it was cheaper for the mobster, whom he didn't identity, to pay him to whack Papalia than to pay the debts. Murdock also alleged that Pat Musitano was trying to get in with the Rizzuto Family boss at the time of Papalia's assassination.

Intriguingly, Murdock claimed to have worked as a hit man for the Musitano brothers and their father Dominic for years. He also claimed to have spared several targets he was ordered to eliminate, including a professional wrestler who used the name Johnny K-9. Murdock said he refused to kill those individuals because they were not part of the Mafia.

THE CALABRIAN MAFIA IN TORONTO: THE SIDERNO GROUP

The story of Toronto's most notorious Mafia group began not in Sicily or in the Canadian metropolis but in a coastal town in Southern Italy. The town was called Siderno, and it was a stronghold of a criminal secret society called the Ndrangheta.

Italy's National Anti-Mafia Directorate now believes that the Ndrangheta is now richer and more powerful than the Sicilian Mafia. Like La Casa Nostra, the Ndrangheta now operates all over the world, and one of its richest, most successful, and most powerful branches is the Toronto-based Siderno Group.

Based in Reggio Calabria, the region of Italy just across the Straights of Messina from Sicily, the Ndrangheta is an international criminal cartel composed of Calabrians that have settled all over the world. Authorities believe the organization targeted Canada because the nation's secretive banking system makes money laundering easy. Since Toronto is the center of Canada's banking system, control of that city is vital to the Ndrangheta's worldwide drug smuggling and money laundering operations.

The name Ndrangheta apparently comes from the Greek word andrangetos, which means a valiant and cunning man. The Ndrangheta's nickname is the "honored society," but its members are all recruited based on family or blood relationships. Overseas Ndrangheta franchises are set up by family members of gangsters back home that moved overseas. Unlike the Mafia, the Ndrangheta functions like a network marketing organization with members operating independently but kicking money back to the bosses.

Italian police believe that there is an "international Ndrangheta movement"; the purpose of the movement is to make as much money as possible for its members. The main motivation for the so called honored society is greed. It functions more like an evil, multilevel marketing scheme than a criminal gang. Members branch out around the world to set up operations and pay for protection and support from the organization.

Its bosses and boards of directors exist largely to settle disputes and divide the spoils rather than direct activities. Individual members have a large degree of independence as long as they make money and pay their share they can do what they want.

Some scholars report that, unlike the Mafia, the Ndrangheta employs women in some of its rackets, such as extortion. There is little evidence that women have participated in Siderno Group activities.

That means the Siderno Group is not really part of the Mafia nor is it a crime family. Instead, it is a group of criminals from the same town in Calabria: Siderno and their many associates. The reason these men are in Canada is twofold: to smuggle drugs and launder money.

The Siderno Group started moving into Canada and increasing its presence as the international drug trade expanded. By the early 21st century some Italian experts believed that the best brains of the organization were operating in Canada. One of the main rackets of the group is to launder profits from cocaine smuggled to Europe and North America from South America.

It is easy to see why Calabrians emigrate abroad in search of opportunity; a December

2008 U.S. diplomatic cable linked to the website Wikileaks described Calabria as a failed state. The same cable accused the Ndrangheta of controlling the area's economy. Control of the Reggio Calabria gives the organization control of the European cocaine trade. Italian officials estimate that 80% of Europe's cocaine is smuggled in through ports in the Reggio Calabria.

Much of the Ndrangheta's power comes from its ability to corrupt authorities. Calabria is so poor that most authorities willingly take its cash. Those who don't, become the targets of violence; an example was Rocco Cassone, an official in a village called Villa San Gionvanni. When he refused to go along with plans to build a bridge between Sicily and Calabria, Cassone had his car set on fire twice, and he received a death threat. Cassone eventually resigned in order to stay alive. The Ndrangheta supported the massive bridge project because it would create lots of graft. Some news reports indicate that Siderno Group members were among those who were posed to profit from the bridge project.

The power extends to Canada; in March 2011 a wiretap placed in a dry cleaning store owned by Ndrangheta boss, or "master," Guiseppe Commisso led to arrests in Canada. Those arrests included one in Toronto and seven in the remote Canadian town of Thunder Bay, Ontario. This incident showed the close connections between the Ndrangheta in Italy and the Siderno Group in Canada.

The arrest of Commisso was part of a crackdown on the Ndrangheta called Project Crimine. Italian authorities told Project Crimine that they unearthed evidence that the

Ndrangheta now has greater drug trafficking and money laundering capabilities than the Mafia. They also believe that the Siderno Group will soon displace the Montreal-based Rizzuto Sicilian Mafia family as the most potent force in Canada's drug trade.

Proof of the Ndrangheta's wealth was demonstrated when police confiscated property belonging to Commisso. The total value of those properties added up to $280 million. Much of the money that bought those properties came from drug money laundered through Toronto by the Siderno Group. Some of the organization's other properties include entire city blocks in Belgium and supermarkets in Germany.

The Siderno Group's origins are clouded in secrecy, but it apparently began in the 1950s when a number of Ndrangheta members immigrated to Toronto. It is unknown how they became familiar with the city, but some of them may have had relatives there. Another possibility is that the gangsters were already familiar with Canada having been held there as prisoners of war during World War II. Tens of thousands of Italian soldiers captured by the British in North Africa were shipped to Canada during the early part of the war.

TORONTO'S CALABRIAN MOB BOSS

The founder and longtime boss of the Siderno Group was probably Cosimo Stalteri, who immigrated to Toronto in 1952. When he moved to Canada, Stalteri already had convictions for assault, carrying an unregistered gun, and theft. Once he arrived in Toronto, Stalteri was appointed to the local La Camera di Controllo, the Ndrangheta's board of directors.

Police became aware of the Siderno Group's existence in 1971 when a wiretap was placed on mob boss Mike Racco's phone. The wiretap led police to Stalteri's house where an initiation ceremony for a new member of the group was held.

Stalteri regularly returned to Italy for visits. During a visit there in 1971 he allegedly killed a street vendor after an argument over a toy. Stalteri was able to return to Canada and live openly in Toronto. The arrest warrant for Stalteri in Italy was cancelled because cops thought he was dead. In Canada, Stalteri masqueraded as a businessman and sensibly avoided publicity and contact with the law.

By 1992 Canadian police learned of a secret Ndrangheta conference in which Stalteri had

been named boss of all ten of Ontario's Ndrangheta clans or families. Stalteri died quietly and
peacefully at a hospital in Toronto at age 86 in
2011. His death was followed by a traditional
mob funeral that included a parade of luxury
cars.

Police apparently discovered the existence
of the Ontario Ndrangheta and the La Camera
di Controllo in 1968. It isn't known how cops
learned of its existence, but the most likely
source was a snitch or rat. The first known
Camera reportedly consisted of Michele, or
Mike, Racco, Salvatore Triumbari, Filippo Vendemini, Rocco Zito, Vicenzo Deleo, Giacomo
Lupino of Hamilton, and Stalteri. Interestingly
enough, Vendemini was murdered in 1969 after
police started monitoring the group's activities.

The Italian Project Crime Report issued in
2010 identifies ten clans or Ndrangheta cells

active in Greater Toronto. These groups make up what is popularly known as the Siderno Group. The leaders of the clans were Vincezo Tavernese, Guiseppe Andriano, Antonio Coluccio, Cosimo Commisso (no word on whether he is related to the master), Angelino Figilomeni, Cosimo Figliomeni, and Vincenzo DeMaria. The report didn't name a boss for the organization. Each of the cells is composed of a member's family or friends from the same village.

Only two of the men listed in the report were wanted by Canadian police. DeMaria was a convicted killer who was arrested on a parole violation in April 2009 and released. Tavernese was arrested in Italy, and Coluccio apparently went underground in Italy in order to avoid arrest.

CHAPTER 4: NOT KNOWN FOR VIOLENCE IN CANADA

Interestingly enough, the Siderno Group is not noted for its violence in Canada, even though the Ndrangheta is very violent in on its home turf. Instead, its members behave themselves and concentrate on money making activities. The clan leaders are apparently smart enough to realize that violence will make them unwelcome in Canada and hinder their ability to make money.

An interesting difference between the Siderno Group and earlier organized crime groups in Canada in the U.S. is its close ties with the homeland. Modern communications and air travel make it possible for the bosses back home to maintain constant contact with gangsters in Canada. The reason there is apparently no Ndrangheta boss in Toronto is that the real leadership is back in Calabria.

The wiretap at Commisso's dry cleaning shop showed that the masters in Calabria were apparently directing the operations in Canada. The Siderno Group is not so much an independent crime family as it is a local subsidiary of an Italian crime syndicate.

A New Mob for a New Century

Unlike earlier generations of Italian mobsters in the U.S. and Canada, the current crop of Sidernos hasn't shown that much interest in street crime. Instead, they seem to be more interested in high-profit international operations, such as drug smuggling and money laundering. Day to day street crime is left to groups like Outlaw Bikers, who are the customers for the group's products.

The Siderno Group appears to be the first 21st century Italian organized crime syndicate in North America. It operates differently from earlier groups and apparently maintains a far lower profile. Online searches reveal that most Canadian news stories about the group focus on the activities of the Ndrangheta back home in Calabria rather than the Toronto beachhead.

The organization's profits seem to be based on activities outside of Canada, such as the cocaine trade between Calabria and South America, rather than crime in Canada. However, the presence of numerous cells throughout Canada indicates a massive, continent-wide smuggling ring reminiscent of the Pizza connection of the 1970s. That could mean one of the Siderno Group's major roles is shipping drugs through Canada to the world's largest drug market—the United States.

Another reason why the Siderno Group has been able to avoid attention is that Canadian law enforcement's attention for the last twenty years has been focused on the Biker War. The RCMP has devoted much of its resources to combatting violent biker gangs, such as the Hells Angels.

There is also a possibility that the Siderno Group might be moving into Montreal, which is the base of the Sicilian Rizzuto Family. The recent mob violence in Montreal, which claimed the lives of most of the Rizzuto Family's leaders and their main rival, Sal "the Iron Worker" Montagna, might provide the Calabrians with the opening they need to take control of Montreal and its important port.

Historically, the Siderno Group was willing to let the Rizzuto Family run the port of Montreal while it ran the drug trade in Ontario. The port of Montreal has long been an important entry point for drugs in North America.

A wild card in the relationship between the Siderno Group and the Rizzuto family might be the recent release of long-time Rizzuto boss, Vic Rizzuto, from prison in the U.S. in October 2012. It remains to be seen whether Vic Rizzuto will strike a new deal with the Ndrangheta or resist its expansion efforts. Most likely the weakened Rizzuto Family will reach some kind of deal with the Calabrians.

THE MAFIA IN THE SUBURBS

The future of the Mafia in Canada probably rests with immigrant criminals from Italy. Instead of independent families in different cities, there will be one national network reporting back to the bosses in Calabria or Sicily. The network will be composed of gangsters imported from Italy whose main focus will be serving the interests of the Italian organization rather than building up an empire in Canada.

Instead of traditional crime centered in the old neighborhood, the next generation Mafiosi will focus on far more lucrative cross-border rackets, such as drug smuggling and money laundering. The new Mafiosi will live in the suburbs in multiethnic neighborhoods rather than in Italian neighbors and live and look much like their neighbors. Since there will be no visible boss and no social club, law enforcement will have a harder time tracking such individuals down.

The Siderno Group rather than historic organizations like the Cotroni Family, the Rizzuto Family, or the Mustiano Family gives us a glimpse of the Canadian Mafia's future. It will be a closely connected network of Italian immigrants dedicated to keeping a low profile while organizing and conducting sophisticated criminal enterprises. Its members will be far more likely to be found at the neighborhood Tim Horton's or watching their sons' hockey games than hanging out at the social club. In other words, the Canadian Mafia will look like the

rest of Canada.

BIBLIOGRAPHY

Amoruso, D. (2011, February 6). The Rat In-
fested Mob . Retrieved January 11, 2013, from
Gangstersinc.ning.com .

Cagnetta, M. (2011, January 9). Fullout war for
supremacy in Montreal's underworld . Retrieved January 10, 2013, from corrietan-
dem.com.

CBC News. (2009, April 15). In Depth Biker Gangs in Canada . Retrieved January 10, 2013, from cbc.ca .

CBC News. (2006, April 11). Mass killings mean Angels win biker turf war: expert. Retrieved January 10, 2013, from cbc.ca.

CBC News. (2009, April 15). Massive police raids target Quebec, N.B. Hells Angels . Retrieved January 11, 2013, from cbc.ca .

Clairmont, S. (2011, November 23). The Weasel and Johnny Pops: a Hamilton Mob Story. Retrieved January 13, 2013, from thespec.com.

CNN. (2007, August 15). Who are the Ndrangheta? Retrieved January 12, 2013, from www.cnn.com.

CTV News. (2011, November 25). High-ranking mobster Salvatore Montagna Murdered.

Retrieved January 10, 2013, from mon-treal.ctavnews.ca.

Edwards, P. (2004, November 26). Frank Co-tronti, 72: Powerful Mobster. Retrieved January 10, 2013, from thestar.com.

Hartley-Parkinson, R. (2011, November 25). Former Mafia boss killed in city where 'he was trying make his to the op'. Retrieved January 10, 2013, from dailymail.co.uk.

Humphreys, A. (2011, February 14). Calabrian Mafia boss earned mob's respect. Retrieved January 12, 2013, from news.nationalpost.com.

Humphreys, A. (1997, July 25). The mafia's war of independence . Retrieved January 11, 2013, from

http://www.nicaso.com/pages/doc_page116.ht
ml.

La Cosa Nostra Database. (n.d.). Agueci Brothers . Retrieved January 11, 2013, from lac-
ndb.com.

La Cosa Nostra Database. (n.d.). Carmen Barillaro. Retrieved Janaury 11, 2013, from
lcandb.com .

La Cosa Nostra Database. (n.d.). Guiseppe Cotroni. Retrieved January 10, 2013, from lac-
ndb.com.

La Cosa Nostra Database. (n.d.). John Papalia .
Retrieved January 11, 2013, from lacndb.com.

La Cosa Nostra Database. (n.d.). Ndrangheta .
Retrieved January 11, 2013, from lacndb.com.

La Cosa Nostra Database. (n.d.). Nicolo Rizzuto. Retrieved January 10, 2013, from lacndb.com.

La Cosa Nostra Database. (n.d.). Paolo Violi. Retrieved January 10, 2013, from lacndb.com.

Lamberti, R. (2010, November 19). Calabrian crime cell operating in Thunder Bay. Retrieved January 12, 2013, from cnews.canoe.ca/CNEWS/Crime .

LaSorte, M. (2004, December). The Ndrangheta Looms Large. Retrieved January 12, 2013, from www.americanmafia.com.

Marzulli, J. (2009, April 14). Bonanno big Salvatore Montagna Booted back to boondocks. Retrieved January 10, 2013, from nydailynews.com.

McAdam, W. I. (n.d.). Organized Crime in Canada. Retrieved January 11, 2013, from the-canadianencyclopedia.com.

Mob News. (2007, March 11). Canada's Musitano Arrested. Retrieved January 11, 2013, from mob-news.blogspot.com .

National Post . (2011, March 18). http://mafiatoday.com/tag/ken-murdock/. Retrieved January 11, 2013, from mafiatoday.com .

National Post . (2007, November 24). Why Italy's Scariest Mob Loves Canada . Retrieved January 12, 2013, from nationalpost.com .

National Post. (2006, November 23). A Humble Begining. Retrieved January 10, 2013, from Canada.com.

National Post. (2007, March 9). Allged parole violations lead to mobster's arrest. Retrieved

January 11, 2013, from canada.com/national-post.

National Post. (2005, July 27). Death among the olive trees. Retrieved January 12, 2013, from canada.com\nationalpost .

Perreaux, L. (2011, November 24). Shot down in a 'sloppy' hit, another Montreal mobster dies . Retrieved January 10, 2013, from theglobe-andmail.com.

Rizzo, A. (2011, March 8). Ndrangheta, Italy's Most Powerful Mafia Organization, Targeted in Cross Border Crackdown . Retrieved January 12, 2013, from www.huffingtonpost.com.

The Associated Press . (2011, March 8). Italy's Mafia crckdown seeks 8 in Canada . Retrieved January 12, 2013, from cbc.ca/news/world.

Thompson, J. (1994, January). Sin Tax Failure: The Market in Contraband Tobacco and Public Safety . Retrieved January 11, 2013, from http://web.archive.org/web/20070415050016/http://www.mackenzieinstitute.com/1994/sin-tax-failure9.htm.

Toledo Blade . (1958, July 2). Crime Inquiry Still Checking on Applachin Meeting. Retrieved January 11, 2013, from google.com\newspapers.

READY FOR MORE?

We hope you enjoyed reading this series. If you are ready to read similar stories, check out other books in the *Organized Crime* series:

Bessie Perri: Queen of the Bootleggers
Rocco Perri was the Al Capone of Canada. Without him, the American market of alcohol would be a little...dry.

Rocco is frequently cited as the most successful bootlegger of Canada, however, for one important reason: his wife, Bessie Perri. If Rocco was the King of Bootlegging, Bessie was the obvious queen.

With page-turning suspense, this gritty book looks at the brains behind Canadian bootlegging and how her cutthroat ways forever changed the landscape of both prohibitions.

The Fighting Parson: The Life of Reverend Leslie Spracklin (Canada's Eliot Ness)

Reverend Spracklin was a gangster's worst nightmare. Known to the press and public as the 'Fighting Parson', he and his handpicked squad of dry agents burst into the roadhouses of Essex County with pistols drawn and fists clenched.

They chased liquor-laden vehicles through dark city streets and along rough country roads, and intercepted rumrunners on the Detroit River in their high-powered speedboat, the Panther II.

The minister went, often alone, into the most dangerous nightspots of 1920s Windsor, and responded to opposition by punching, not preaching.

He thought nothing of carrying around a stack of blank search warrants and filling them out himself as needed. He could not be scared or bought, and he survived one assassination attempt after another. It was only when a roadhouse owner who also happened to be a long-time enemy died at his hands that the campaign was finally stopped.

His life is told in this short book.

Bloody Valentine: The Bloody History of the Saint Valentine's Day Massacre

The Saint Valentine's Day Massacre is one of the most notorious murders of all time.

In the crime-ridden Chicago of the Prohibition era, gangsters like Al Capone battled for power, but few went to the extreme lengths that Capone did on that fateful day in 1929.

This short book gives you an exciting look at one of the most notorious criminals of all time, and the massacre he masterminded to finally gain control of the bootleg liquor trade.

Pray he has chocolates in that box and not a Tommy gun! This is one Valentine's Day you will never forget.

Public Enemy #1: The Biography of Alvin Karpis--America's First Public Enemy

Before John Dillinger, Pretty Boy Floyd, and Baby Face Nelson made the term "Public Enemy" famous, there was Alvin Karpis--one of the ruthless leaders of the Barker-Karpis gang.

It was him that J. Edgar Hoover first thought worthy of the title Public Enemy

In a page-turning style, this true crime book traces his criminal orgins from his young days as a bootlegger to his ultimate demise.

The Real Gangs of New York

The subject of a classic history by Herbert Asbury and an Academy Award nominated film by Martin Scorsese, the gangs of The Five Points in New York have become the stuff of legend. But how much is legend and how much is fact?

In this short book we examine the original gangs of the Five Points in New York and see how accurate the film was (spoiler alert: not very) and what Asbury may have gotten wrong in his original research on this era.

From the Bowery Boys to the Dead Rabbits, we look at the gangs that operated not just in the Five Points, but also those who wanted a piece of the action there and engaged in gang wars that would leave even modern thugs quivering in their boots!

Sam the Cigar: A Biography of Sam Giancana

Sam Giancana is one of the most famous gangsters in U.S. history, with rumored links to the CIA and President Kennedy.

 But was he really involved in the assassination attempt on Fidel Castro and the assassination of J.F.K.?

This thrilling bio gives you all the details on one of America's most fascinating underworld figures.

Newsletter Offer

Don't forget to sign up for your newsletter to grab your free book:

http://www.absolutecrime.com/newsletter

Made in United States
North Haven, CT
17 January 2022

14900515R00057